Grief and New Graves

Edward "Little Man" Lewis

OVER THE EDGE BOOKS

OVER THE EDGE BOOKS

Grief and New Graves
© Copyright at Edward Lewis
2015 Over The Edge Publishing

ISBN 978-0-9907110-9-4

Book layout by Andrew C. Edman

Printed in the United States of America

http://overtheedgebooks.com/

Rarely do we get to experience a voice as raw as Lil Man's. His story is one of anger, passion, loss, redemption, fear and forgiveness. His story is all too common yet unique at the same time.
I learned from this and enjoyed it.

-Talib Kweli

Grief and New Graves is a powerful testimony about the harsh world our youth of today are navigating.
A Must read for all parents, no matter the color.

-Bun B

This is the story of a true leader that was raised on the north side of Houston, Texas.
How did a young kid who was into sports get involved in a life of gangs and violence?
My mother always told me that living that lifestyle I would end up dead or in prison.

I should have listened to my mother!!!

SHOUTOUTS

To my mother Linda Lewis and my sisters
Arlinda Killings , Cynthia Bonier, and Kimberly Flanagan
and to my brother Devon Lewis.

I love y'all for being there for me.

REST IN PEACE

To my homies Crazy J., Dampe, and Rene "Fruit" Tijerina:
I will never forget the love and loyalty we had for each other.

INTRODUCTION

People ask me why I became a writer. I didn't write this to be thought of as a "writer." I wrote this book because there are far too many deaths, imprisonments, and innocent victims that gang violence has been the cause of. This book is dedicated to the young people who feel they have no choice but to join gangs and to the many families that are destroyed by gang violence.

Growing up in Houston, I was known as Little Man, the leader of the Crip Cartel. I've seen the pain that death causes, I've felt the hurt caused by the death of someone's family member, friend or loved one. My past experience as a gang leader has given me the ability to put this book together. God willing, after reading this book, joining a gang will no longer be an option for you. However, this book is not only for kids or gang members; it's also for parents and anyone who realizes the toll the vicious cycle of gang violence has taken on our communities.

My Brother Devon and I

GRIEF AND NEW GRAVES

CHAPTER ONE

My Lindale Little League Baseball team

My story begins on August 12th, 1974 in Houston, Texas. As a baby, I always looked like a little man, so "Little Man" is what I was called. I struggle to recall my early childhood memories, but I do remember my mom telling me that she and my dad separated when I was about three years old. I do not know where they met, but my father is from Louisiana and my mother is from Texas. Louisiana and Texas folk have always had an interesting connection.

My mother's name is Linda Lewis, and she raised five kids by herself. I am my dad's only son. I have three sisters and one brother, and I love them very much. My oldest sister is Cynthia Bonier, the second oldest is Gayle Killings, then there is me. Later down the line comes my little brother Devon Lewis, and finally my baby sister, Kimberly Flanagan. I was the only boy and the baby of the family for a long time, so of course my mother spoiled me. My sister Gayle was my protector. She used to take care of me and watch me while my mother was at work. My mother worked daily to support her children, and she did a hell of a job. Never once did we go without food, clothing or shelter. There where even times where she would bring us to her job because she couldn't find a babysitter. Linda Lewis is a strong, beautiful Black woman that has lead a life of struggle, but she never let it break her. She dealt with abusive men at times. I used to see her boyfriends hitting her, but I was too little to help. She always told me, never hit a woman, and now that I am older I realize she was speaking with pain.

The north side of Houston, where I grew up, is a mixture of Blacks and Mexicans, with the Mexicans outnumbering the Blacks. There are places in this country where that would cause problems but on the north side we all stuck together. My family lived in an apartment complex called Irvington Court. I was a little skinny boy who loved attention but was too shy to go looking for it. Quietness was my strategy. I would let everyone else do all the talking until people noticed that I was a little different from my friends. There were times when that worked too well. People used to come up to me and ask if I was alright, because I wasn't really talking. I have always had strong emotions, but I was pretty good at hiding them.

The Mexicans dominated the neighborhood and they loved baseball, so my mother put me in Little League when I was in second grade. I was one of just two black kids on the team, the rest of the kids were Mexican. In fact, we may have been the only two Blacks in the whole League. My neighborhood was full of dope fiends, so it was important to my mother that I occupied my time with constructive activities.
I began to love baseball, and the team camaraderie helped me to become very comfortable around the Mexicans. They treated me like I was part of their family. I had no brothers at the time, so just being around this group of boys made me feel like I did. My mother couldn't make it to my games too often, I think she made it to about two of them. She was always busy working trying to feed us, so I wasn't upset because I knew it was hard for her. My dad just never came around at all, and I had no idea where he was. My teammates would buy me food and drinks after the games when my mother could not afford to. Once, a teammate named Armando's mom even bought me a pair of cleats that matched my uniform. You should have seen how happy I was! The cleats were actually too small for my growing feet, but I was so grateful to receive them that I didn't tell anybody. I'd just squeeze into them and play. My feet would hurt after each game, but I just kept on playing in them. I really don't know why I never told anyone that the cleats were too small, but I was probably afraid they would try to take them back and the store wouldn't have my size. Whenever somebody gave me something I always truly appreciated it, no matter what it was.

I played baseball for four years straight and became very good at it. I used to pitch, play catcher and centerfield. When I wasn't playing baseball, I used to play marbles under a tree with some friends of mine. I was one of the best marble shooters in Irvington Court. I love to compete but I've never been a sore loser. I just figure out how I lost the first time and try not to repeat that mistake.

While I was excelling on the baseball diamond, excelling at school life was a different challenge. The sixth grade was one of my hardest years. I was a new student and fresh meat for the bullies. I had to fight often, and was always in defense mode. I became very aggressive. One day while walking thru the halls someone thru a ball of paper at me. I turned around and hit the first person I saw looking at me right in the face. I didn't know who threw that paper, I just knew someone had to pay for it. This kid was wearing glasses, and when I hit him they shattered and cut his face. The parents tried to press charges, but the school convinced them not to. I dodged that bullet but my mother was mad as hell. Believe me, I got my butt whipped for that one. Later I found out that the kid I hit lived right around the corner from Irvington Court. I ended up apologizing for what I did and we became pretty good friends. I've never had a problem apologizing if I was in the wrong, which I certainly was. Even though the beginning of the sixth grade school year was rough, by the end of it I had a lot of friends.

Every Saturday morning while most kids my age were watching cartoons, I was watching kung fu movies. For me they were about more than just a bunch of people fighting. My favorites were Five Deadly Venoms, The Kid With The Golden Arms and Shaolin Masters. These movies dealt with themes that were becoming important to me as a young man, things like loyalty among friends, passion, and love. Even though these movies were poorly over dubbed in English, there was a lot of knowledge in them. For many kids growing up in the hood, kung fu movies become the introduction to a code of honor. To this day I still love watching those movies. They lead me to getting involved in martial arts at an early age. In junior high school I studied Shaolin kung fu for a little awhile. It taught me that inner strength comes from within. This was a lesson I would have to apply later in life.

My days of playing baseball came to an abrupt end in the seventh grade. One day while at school my side started hurting out of nowhere. I went to the nurse's office but they had no answers. She let me lay down and rest for a while, then she told me to go home and get some more rest. It was a Friday, and my mother went fishing on Friday. My sisters were also out, at their Dad's house. My mother would sometimes let my friends stay over and that night I was up late watching movies with two of them. All of a sudden my side started to hurt again, but much worse. It hurt so bad I damn near started to cry. My mother was still out fishing, so I had to call my dad. My friends waited with me until he came to pick me up then they went home. Fortunately, my dad's wife was a nurse and insisted that I go to the hospital. It took the doctors a half an hour to decide that I needed my appendix removed. When I finally did speak to my mother she was upset at herself for not being there for me when I was in so much pain, but I let her know it wasn't her fault because I never told her about my side hurting while I was in school. Picking me up that night and making sure I got to the hospital was the only good thing I could say my dad ever did for me at that time.

As I hit puberty I became very popular at school. I had both the Black and the Mexican girls wanting to date me. I was real stuck up back then, so I'd laugh at them with my friends. I never liked to date girls that stayed in the same projects as I did. It was normal for most of the boys and girls in Irvington Court to date each other, and it created a cycle where generations of families would be stuck living there. I never wanted to be stuck in that lifestyle so I searched for girls outside my projects. I was a free spirit, and a little bit of an outcast because I did my own thing.

One of my earliest partners from around the way was a Mexican dude named Chino. Chino used to hang around this gang called the Play Boys, and when I began to hang with Chino I began to talk and walk like a gangster. I never became part of that gang but I was definitely affiliated. I used to ride around and sell dope with them. They took me to a lot of parties. I used to always bring a couple of black friends with me, so they could see what it was like to go to a Mexican party. I was like a bridge between my Black friends and my Mexican friends, but my Black friends would never leave the projects. They would just hang around selling dope, gambling and talking to the same girls. I was different. I moved around, I never limited myself to Irvington Court. Even so, I felt that my Black friends truly understood me in a deeper way, and they were always there when I needed them whether I hung around the way or not. My crew was made up of good dudes like Johnny "Lil J", Joseph "Fu-Fu", James, Tyrone, and the rest the I.V.P's, which stood for Irvington Village Posse. My Mexican friends had a lot of love for me too, and it was mutual. Dudes like Jose "Lil Pep", Chris "Chongo", and George "Green Eyes". would do anything for me, and I would do anything for them. These people showed me the importance of having good friends.

CHAPTER TWO

Marshall Middle School on Houston's north side was my zone junior high school, so that's where I went when I was a pre-teenager. The school was mostly Mexicans, with a few Blacks and even fewer Whites, and going there was no picnic. At Marshall you had to be tough or else you were going to get bullied every day. The area surrounding the school was poverty stricken and crime ridden and the student body reflected these problems. There were daily gang fights after school, so linking up with the right crew was essential to survival.

Hanging with Chino and the Play Boys got me into a lot of trouble, but it also built up my reputation among the Mexicans. We thought we were the baddest gangsters ever. I remember this one time when another Mexican dude took a liking to Chino's little sister, which Chino did not approve of. When Chino threatened to shoot this guy, the guy left Chino's sister alone. No one took Chino for a joke because he always carried a gun with him, so I began to carry one as well. I had this .22 pistol that I carried everywhere I went, and I wasn't scared to use it. The Play Boys had a lot of enemies, and their enemies became my enemies. Gunfights in the street were not uncommon. The sad part about it was often I didn't even know what my enemy looked like, I just used to hear gun shots coming at me from a distance. I had to adapt to this way of life very fast, and paranoia became my friend. I used to walk against the flow of traffic so I could see the cars coming towards me. The sound of brakes, doors slamming, and loud crashes used to make me reach for my gun, which I tucked in my pants under my shirt.

I couldn't dodge bullets forever. One night when Chino and I ventured into an unfamiliar hood to talk to some girls, I got shot. I heard the shots first, and as we took of running, a bullet hit me in the leg. I immediately fell to the ground, but fear and adrenaline got me back up and running just as quickly as I had fallen. We eventually made it back to our hood, but I was bleeding from a bullet hole in my right leg. I went to the hospital, received an I.V., a couple of shots, and left to go hang out with Chino again the same night. I was more worried about my mother finding out I got shot and about her having to pay the hospital bill than I was about my own well being. I initially tried to hide my wound from my mother, but I wasn't walking straight. When she asked me about my leg, I lied and told her that I tried to climb a fence and my leg got caught on a wire that was sticking out. Do you think she believed me? Hell no!!! It took her one look at the two holes I had in my leg, the one in the front and the one in the back because the bullet went straight through, for her to know it was a gunshot wound. She was scared for my life, but she was also very upset and disappointed with me because she didn't raise me to be wilding in the street. She raised me better and she knew I was a good kid.

As soon as my leg healed up, there I was back on the street hanging with the same group of people. They even showed me more respect now than before. I became known as a gangster from the north side and my reputation preceded me. Just my nickname alone, "Little Man", would get people's attention. I remember going to the mall one day with "Little Man" on the back of my shirt. Two girls who were walking past me saw my name on the shirt and whispered "that's Little Man" in hushed tones like I was a celebrity. They kept looking at me as if they wanted to say something to me. I didn't know them so I kept on walking.

Eventually things started to sour between me and the Play Boys. They were getting jealous of the recognition Chino and I were getting and it seemed like their frustrations would bubble to the top soon. One day after Chino and I gave one of the leaders of the Play Boys a ride home, they put us to the test. When we arrived at the house there were already a couple of members of the Play Boys standing in the front yard. The leader of the Play Boys that we were with had a brother that was second in command at the time, and when we got out of the car the brother started an argument with Chino. The argument quickly became a physical fight with the Play Boys cheering on their boy to win. It was only right for me to cheer on my boy Chino in that situation, so that's what I did. The Play Boys leader who Chino and I had just driven home with was close enough to hit me in the face, so that's what he did. We both pull out our guns, but mine wasn't cocked, so I thought on my feet and talked him into fist fighting me instead. We fought for a while until I started to get the best of him. When his boys saw that, one of them ran into the house and came back out with a rifle, which he shot into the air for effect. At that point, Chino and I got back into the car and drove off. That was the start of a real beef between us and the Play Boys. The fight I had with the leader of the Play Boys got me even more respect in my hood because a lot of people were scared of him. I became an urban legend. The word on the streets was that I beat up the leader of the Play Boys.

One night while I was walking to Chino's house, I ran into the leader of the Play Boys again. This time he was by himself and wanted to fight me again. We went at it again in the middle of the Greenspoint Baptist Church parking lot. I was kicking his butt again, so he pulled out a knife on me. This was the rare day that I did not carry my gun, so I backed away and told him that we were past fist fights in the street; it was time for war. Later on at Chino's house I told him what had happened, so Chino let me borrow his gun for my walk back home. As soon as I got home guess who was waiting for me? The brother of the leader of the Play Boys was sitting on my front porch. I braced myself because I thought he wanted trouble, but he actually wanted to apologize for his brother for pulling out a knife on me. He came to tell me his brother didn't want any more trouble with me and to let everything go. My reputation was now working in my favor.

The beginning of the eighth grade is when my life really changed. I had so much respect in the hood I felt like it belonged to me. Even though I technically owned no property, I felt like the schools, the stores, the parks and the streets were mine. The summer after my eighth grade year I got involved with a gang called the Crazy Crips. They represented Fifth Ward, Greenspoint, and the north side of Houston. By the time I started at Houston's Jefferson Davis High School in the 9th grade I was a full fledged member of the Crazy Crips. People normally associated the Crips with the west coast but there were gang members from California who either moved to or went to jail in Texas that brought the Blood and Crip culture with them. We used to walk down the halls of the school in large groups as a show of strength, but others would still try to test us. It was only two weeks into the school year when a group of guys walked up to me and said "you think you bad!" I responded by saying "you don't even know me fool", and as my crew of Crips advanced towards them the retreated to a van and drove off. What made this particular incident stick out in my mind was the fact that one of the guys in the group that stepped to me was a friend. I knew him from my hood, and once I even stopped him from getting beat up by a group of Mexicans by telling them he was with me. I was mad that he would betray me like that. Later that night I talked to the crew about what happened and became even more upset as I recounted the story.

The incident with these guys was still heavy on my mind when I woke up to go to school the next morning. I had to decide whether or not it was worth it to bring my gun to school with me. Do I take the risk of getting jumped and losing, or do I make sure everyone knows how gangster I thought I was? I made a choice, and the choice I made was ultimately the wrong one. I took my gun to school. As soon as I seen one of those guys I walked right up to him and asked "what was that all about yesterday when you and your friends came up to me?" At first, he said it's over with and that they ain't tripping anymore, so I walked away. This must have made this guy think that I wasn't serious when I stepped to him. As I headed back towards my gang he blurted out "what the hell you want to do?" When I turned back around, I could see that his boys had joined his side, which is what made him change his original tune. I waved at my gang, and we all started running towards these guys. We began to fight ferociously right in front of the school. During the brawl, one of the other guys found a stick and came at me like he was about to hit me with it. I quickly pulled out my gun and shot him in the leg. All of the students started running around panicked in every direction. Knowing I had to get low, I went to one of my friend's house for a few hours.

At three o'clock I started walking home. I decided to pretend I was coming home from school so my mother wouldn't trip. On my way home I was trailed by a police car. I still had my gun on me so I had to think fast. I saw a friend of mine on a bike and I asked him to give me a ride home because the cops were after me. He agreed, and he held my gun for me. However, the police showed up at my front door early the next morning anyway. They put me in the back of a squad car, took me to school and questioned me about what happened. I didn't cooperate much so they took me to juvenile detention and gave me a court date. My mom tried to get me out so I could stay with her until my day in court, but the judge refused, saying that he didn't want me going back to the same environment. My dad came to get me instead, they only let him because he lived in a different neighborhood, Acres Homes, and because he agreed to take me to a counselor. I began to go back to school, but after two weeks the counselor convinced my dad to put me in something called treatment counseling at Hermann Hospital. When I got to the facility with my dad and the counselor, they put me in a room and locked the door behind me. As I realized what was happening, I started beating on the door. I was being tricked, they were going to leave me here. At that moment two big fat men grabbed me and tried to subdue me, but that took a long time. I was hurt, confused and very angry by what was happening to me.

I was taken to another room and locked in there until I calmed down some more. For three months I stayed there, spending my days with strangers talking about their problems in a circle. Every time it was my turn to talk I said nothing because I didn't think I had a problem. Upon release I was sent back to live with my dad until my court date. I was very upset at my dad for doing me like that. I felt that he wasn't man enough to tell me the truth about where he was taking me, so I began to harbor resentment for him.

I started going back to Jefferson Davis again. I was hanging out with my Crip gang, but I wasn't getting into any trouble. Things seemed like they were looking up until my dad started talking crazy to me. One night we got into a bad argument that started about some food I didn't finish but escalated until we got into all of the unspoken issues we were having. He talked bad about my mother and said things to me like since he brought me into this world, he would take me out of this world. At that point I told myself that living with him was unhealthy. I needed to get out of there immediately and that's exactly what I did. I walked out, caught a bus back to my mother's house and told her what happened. After a couple of days I called him and let him know I was alright.

My day in court finally arrived. Considering the things I did like going to school, treatment counseling and generally staying out of trouble, I thought the judge might cut me a break. But those things meant nothing to him; he still sent me to a juvenile correctional facility called Crockett State School that was run by the Texas Youth Commission for a year. The Texas Youth Commission is supposed to help rehabilitate young people so that they don't revert to old habits, but as soon as I got there, I had a couple of fights. It took about a month for me to settle in and get used to how it worked. My mom never came to visit me, but I would call her all the time. I know it was hard for her to come because of work and having to raise her other kids so I was never mad at her. My dad came to see me sometimes and when it was time for me to get released, he picked me up and took me to my mom's house. My family was so happy to see me when I got home.

It was crazy to see how much things had changed in one year. My homeboy Chino was on the run for murder. Word on the street was that he killed one of our old friends. I don't know how what happened but whatever problem they had started, ended badly. Not only was the victim a friend from around the way, but he also had a wife and kids, which made me sad. I was growing up too quickly.

I began to hear rumors in my hood that the guy I shot was looking for me. I decided to buy a new gun off the streets to protect myself. I fell back into the habit of carrying it with me everywhere I went, to the mall, to the store, to parties and even to the damn library. When I was in my house lying down looking at T.V. it was right there under the couch where I can reach for it quickly. Houston Texas is a gun culture. You can get one damn near anywhere. I never pulled it out or pointed it at anyone unless I had to, but everyone knew I carried a gun.

After I left T.Y.C. I moved back to the north side and got my GED. Instead of going back into the public school system I thought it was best to go to school for a trade. I was sixteen years old at the time, I started taking up word processing at PolyTech Institute. It was a six month class, but I left after four. By this time I had developed a real problem with authority figures and really did not like people telling me what to do. On the last day that I spent there I had an argument with a teacher about a bus token. Usually, the teacher gave me my token when I finished my work. On this day the teacher decided to hold my tokens until the entire class was finished. I didn't understand why this time was different and I felt that the teacher was picking on me because I was the youngest person in the class. Later on the school's principal gave me the token and said "don't worry about the argument, you can go home," but I never really felt comfortable there and I used this issue as an excuse to not go back. I didn't think I belonged there. It was a small argument that led to a big decision. I started hanging back on the streets with my friends, nothing to do, nowhere to go.

Back in the mix, I found out an interesting piece of information. It turned out that the guy I shot was a good friend of one of my friends, and they were both members of the Rollin 60's Crips. I called my friend one night to hang out, but the dude he asked to come pick me up recognized my name. "Little Man from the North Side? That's the guy that shot me." My friend suggested that me and the guy I shot fight one on one, no guns, no one jumps in, and settle this problem once and for all. He also told me the guy I shot wasn't worried about it, fed me some line about letting the "past be the past." I didn't trust it at all, and now I no longer trusted my friend. I told him I would see him later and went to hang out with some other homies.

As I got older I got wiser, but instead of using that knowledge to get out of the streets, I applied it to running the streets more efficiently. I began to trust people less and less but at the same time I expanded the Crazy Crips into other neighborhoods and brought more guys into my gang. Things started to change quickly in the streets. I brought in a bunch of guys from another neighborhood to join my gang. Under my leadership the Crazy Crips changed into the Crip Cartel and became far more organized. We even came up with an acronym for the word cartel; **C**aring **A**nd **R**espect **T**ogether **E**quals **L**ove. That's what we stood for and that's how I kept us united. With this newfound organizational structure, we became one of the biggest Crip gangs in Houston. Our reach and influence stretched across Houston, our name rang bells in Greenspoint, the north side, Height, northwest, northeast, southeast, and 5th Ward.

We did a lot of things, some good and some bad. We sold drugs, stole cars, committed robbery and had gang fights, but we also had certain street codes that we strictly adhered to. We first and foremost protected our community from rival gangs. We enforced rules in our community like no stealing and no graffiti on schools, libraries and private property. There were folks in the community who saw us as a positive influence rather than a negative one. I used to have parents come ask me to talk to their kids about staying in school and staying out of trouble.

CHAPTER THREE

The Crip Cartel continued to grow and eventually became targeted by the gang task force set up by Houston police on the north side of Houston. Those task force cops used to harass us all the time. We could just be playing basketball in the park or having a barbecue with our families when they would show up, start patting us down and threaten to lock us up. One time I was at a park with my wife and son when they pulled me over, searched me, and took me to jail for littering when they couldn't find anything. I was mad as hell because I didn't do anything wrong, I was just having a day out with my family. The harassment got progressively worse until it reached the point where I couldn't even go to the store with my mom without getting pulled over. The task force didn't care that I was with my mom, they brought me in on trumped up charges like "resisting arrest." They claimed that I ran from them when they tried to arrest me, and it was my word against theirs.

Here I was back in a jail cell. However, I was no longer a little kid, I was on the verge of manhood and the stakes were getting higher. I had a family of my own, and that began to factor into my decision making. I was due for a life changing experience, and it happened when homicide detectives paid me a visit. First they asked me if I was Little Man from Crip Cartel, then they told me that some man got robbed and killed in my neighborhood. They said my name was brought up and they asked me if I had something to do with it. I told them that I didn't know what they were talking about, that I had nothing to do with anyone getting robbed and killed. Then the questioning got more intense and started to feel like an interrogation. They asked about my whereabouts on August 11th and August 12th of that year and if I wore a blue rag on my head. That's when I knew they had nothing on me; I never wore a rag on my head, that makes you an easy target for a rival gang. Also on both August 11th and 12th I was at my homeboys house with a lot of people. I remembered clearly because August 12th is my birthday and we were having a party. My alibi was rock solid. With nothing left to blame me for, the homicide detectives told me that I needed to find out who committed the crime and tell them or else they were going to charge me with it. I had nothing to do with that crime, so I just waited it out and was never charged. I couldn't shake the feeling that somebody in my own gang set me up for the fall.

That was the moment that I decided I wasn't going to gang bang anymore. The trust and the loyalty that once drew me to the gang life was no longer there. Maybe it was never there in the first place. I was only 19 and I wanted to live the rest of my life as a family man. I had three beautiful kids, two girls and a boy. My oldest daughter's name is Emry R. Lewis. Her mother's name is Christine. We are not together but we broke up on good terms and remain partners in raising Emry. Later on I got involved with another woman named Erica. We got married and had two kids, my son Edward G. Lewis III and my youngest daughter, Destiny N. Lewis. My family is my biggest inspiration and I wanted to be around for them. I didn't want to have to try and be a father from jail cell.

When I got out of jail and got back up with the Crip Cartel, I told them what I went thru and that I was thru with banging for good. I had a Crip Cartel party at my house so I could announce who would be their new leader. Everything went smooth that night and I felt like I was putting my gang banging days behind me. For awhile after I left the gang I would still go visit them to see how they were doing and to give them some advice if they needed it. I was treated like an O.G., but that would come with a heavy price.

Once again, in the blink of an eye, my life would change. My wife and I decided to go riding around one Friday night. That's what we did in Houston, it's a car culture, so we ride. Knowing that I would be coming home late, I decided to take my rifle with me for protection. I put it in the trunk, and off we went, riding around the neighborhood. Soon, I stopped to talk to some friends I saw talking in the parking lot in front of their apartment buildings. Another friend of mine drove up and asked us if we wanted to go to the club with him. It was his birthday. It was already late and the club was far, but my wife really wanted to go and I hadn't taken her out in awhile. My homeboy had his wife with him, so when she suggested we ride with them, I put my rifle in the trunk of his car and we rode out to the club. We never made it inside because as soon as we pulled up, the club got raided for god knows why. There were police cars all over the place. The club was being shut down and everybody inside had to leave. As I began to head back to my homeboys car with my wife I heard people behind me cursing and saying "Crip killer." At first I didn't think it was me they were talking to until I turned around and made eye contact. The words were coming from a group of guys that were following me. As they got closer, I stood between them and my wife and told her to get in the car so that nothing would happen to her. Soon enough they were standing right in front of me, cursing me out. I had no idea what their problem was with me specifically or where they knew me from. I told the main guy, the one doing the most of the cursing, to fight me one on one without help from his punk friends. He wasn't going for that, so we just stood there cussing each other out, until the police came over and broke it up. I got in the car with my wife and friends and we drove off.

We pulled into a nearby parking lot. I got my rifle out of the trunk and put it in my lap. We jumped on the freeway to head home and call it a night. Because it was so late, the freeway was mostly empty, except for two cars my wife spotted which were filled with the same group of guys that had just stepped to me outside of the club. I decided to shoot first and talk later. I shot at those cars about 25 times, until I was out of ammunition. The car I hit the most pulled onto the side of the freeway while the other car began to chase us. We lost them on the freeway, made it to my homeboy's apartment where I picked up my car and headed home with my wife.

The next day my wife and I went to my sister's house to visit, and the news was on while we were there. All of a sudden I saw one of the cars I shot at on the side of freeway. The news reporter was saying that there was a shoot out and that one of the guys in that car was shot and killed. I called around the hood to see if anyone knew who the guy who died was. I found out he was a member of a rival gang called the North Side Aztecs that didn't stay too far from us. The North Side Aztecs would have definitely known who I was, that's why they kept saying "Crip killer" outside of the club. The news reporter also said that the guy I killed was very young, so my guess was he stepped to me thinking he would get respect for stepping to the leader of the Crip Cartels. Little did he know I wasn't the leader anymore!
It didn't take long for word to get out on the street that I had killed a North Side Aztec. I had people calling me asking if it was true. Homicide was hunting for me. They showed up at my house early the next morning and took my wife and I down to the station. They wanted a statement of what happened that night from both of us. I was hesitant to give a statement, but when the police told me they had one from my wife I wrote one immediately. They let my wife go but they locked me up that day on charges of murder and aggravated assault. Later that same day I got out on bond and hired a lawyer.

When I went to court, I plead self-defense. My trial lasted for five days. At first I thought it was looking good, but at some point it seemed like my lawyer stopped fighting for me and things went downhill fast. I told my lawyer I wanted to take the stand and tried to take my defense into my own hands. I felt that was the only way to save myself from getting a life-sentence. I got up on the stand and told the jury the truth; I thought my life and the lives of my wife and friends were in jeopardy so I took steps to defend us. The jury found me guilty of manslaughter and aggravated assault and gave me 20 years. I was locked up in 1998 and release in 2013 after serving 15 years. My wife divorced me the moment I received my sentence, and none of my friends ever wrote me a letter. While I was locked up, I decided to write down my thoughts for those who wonder what my life has been like, for those who respected me and for those who hated me. Living the life of a gangster is not easy.

Now that I am home, I want to stay home for my family. When I was younger, I lived recklessly and took life for granted. The gangster lifestyle will eventually make you realize that life is short. Your life can be taken or dramatically altered in an instant, so you have to stop and smell the roses sometimes. Life is not just about working to pay the rent, surviving. It's about living. It took me going to prison for 15 years to realize that.

CHAPTER FOUR

As I sat in that prison observing my surroundings, I saw all types of inmates walking back and forth. Their similarities however, seemed stronger than their differences. Most of them had a lot of time, but you wouldn't know unless they told you. They all looked so innocent, smiling and laughing with each other. They showed respect towards each other as if they were upstanding citizens, not criminals. Most of them were men of color, like me, who couldn't have been older than 35 years old. Despite our individual characteristics, we were all criminalized from birth. We came from the poorest neighborhoods and the schools we went to operated as direct pipelines into the prison system. It was like slavery all over again. As those inmates walked back and forth past me I couldn't help but to notice their different tattoos. Some of them had tattoos that seemed like art for art's sake, but most of the tattoos people have in prison are gang related. The longer you are incarcerated, the more that feeling of power you get from being in a gang seems to fade away. No longer do you smile at your tattoos with delight when you see them because the reasons you had for joining a gang have vanished once you get locked up.

The question of why we even join gangs continued to weigh heavy on my mind. It seems to have been asked over and over again by our community, law enforcement and politicians. But do they really want us to have the answer? How is a gang different than the police? What's more gangster than bombing another country to advance your political beliefs or economic advancement? Our leaders point to smaller reasons for gang violence but never the root cause. To identify the main reason they would have to stop blaming victims and examine their own behavior. It is up to us in the community to identify the main reasons. Once we do that, we can stop our children from wanting to be gang members.

Too often we focus on the gang as a whole and not the gang members individually. We want to eliminate the whole gang with one blow, and that's never going to happen. Many of the O.G.s already have criminal records and are stuck in the system; we need to focus on the kids who are joining gangs for the first time. Usually when an O.G. decides to leave his gang it's because he is tired of the trouble that comes with the lifestyle and he has found something different to live for. But for every O.G. that leaves there are five new kids joining who have no clue about the trouble coming their way. Five new gang members for one O.G. with an existing criminal record is a trade any gang will take anytime. This is how gangs evolve and continue to grow, it's a cycle. It's always good to see someone get out of a gang, but it's great to have them not even join one from the start.

We have to start with the children. They are the future for the gangs, but we need them to be the future for the community. We have to get to them before the gangs do. We must educate our children about the consequences of gang violence, especially in communities with a lot of gangs. We must not be afraid to talk with our kids early about gangs. As soon as our kids start school or go playing in the park they will be exposed to gangs and begin to learn on their own. At least one gang member will try and talk to your child about his gang. It's better for children to be prepared for this talk. Our children are targeted by these gangs, but knowledge makes them a harder target to hit.

I am writing from experience. Being an ex-gang leader, I have seen kids come into the gang right as the O.G.'s leave. It's a vicious cycle that must be disrupted. I truly believe that the large majority of kids who join gangs do it because they want to be part of a family that they can call their own. This comes from a lack of direction, attention or love. It is also human nature to want to be part of a club. The same mentality exists in sports or politics. It's like playing for a football team or deciding to become a democrat or a republican.

This is how it works. A family might give the child attention and love, but no direction. So when a kid is at school, at the park or just in the neighborhood, he gets his direction from those surroundings. Gang members can come in and provide direction. They can start influencing a child to think that this life style is all that matters, and the child begins to think this is the correct direction. It's like brainwashing, and brainwashing doesn't happen overnight.

Another family may give their child direction and love, but not enough attention. A lack of attention can make a child feel lonely and unnoticed. This can be a very serious problem because a child always wants his parent's attention, even if the child is unable to express that. This same child will seek attention from outside the home if he or she does not receive it from the parents. When this happens, who do you think is out there waiting for these children? Gang members. The child is looking for attention and the gangs are looking for new members, so the gangs give the child all the attention they want. Gang members invite them to parties, take them to the mall and talk with them about their problems. The gang starts to make the child feel good about getting the attention they were lacking and having a group to belong to. All of this happens before the child is even asked to join the gang, so when that day comes, the answer is usually "yes."

There is another scenario where a family might give a child direction and attention, but not enough love. Many parents believe that attention is the same as love, but I'm here to tell you it is not. Attention can be positive or negative, love is always positive. Attention without love is empty. When the child doesn't feel the love at home, the child will go looking for it outside of the home. Gang members often describe the love they give to and receive from one another. After hearing this over and over, a child will think this love is real and want it for themselves. Even though this love is not real, it feels real to the child. I call the love between gang members "imitation love", because most gang members don't love each other, they just use each other. But our children don't know any other kind of love so they believe in the love the gang members profess. Who is to blame here? Gang members? Gang leaders? Parents for not giving our children the things they need physically and emotionally? At this point it doesn't matter who's to blame, so let's stop pointing fingers. Let's disrupt the cycle by connecting with our children early. They need attention, direction and love in equal measure.

LIL' MAN

Crazy J and I

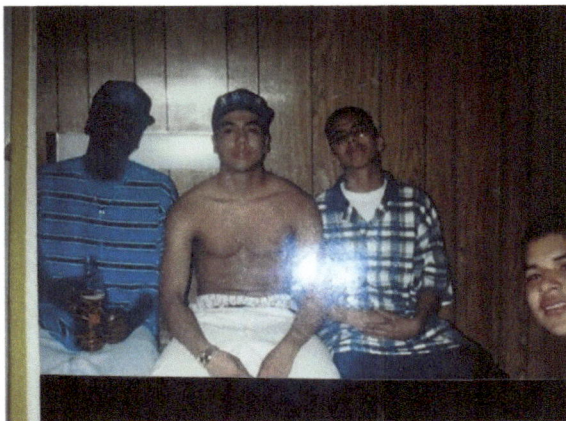

Ex-Crip Cartel Hanging Out With Ex-NSCP

Carlos, My Son Lil' Edward and I, Crazy J and His Daughter Danielle

My Homeboy Dampi. R.I.P

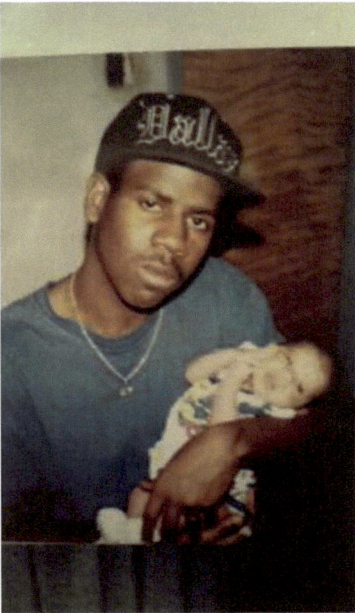

My Son Lil Edward and I

The Crip Cartels Chilling with Members of NSCP

My Irvington Village Family, IVP and I

My Mother Linda and I.

Hanging with My Homies From IVP

My North Side Homies and I

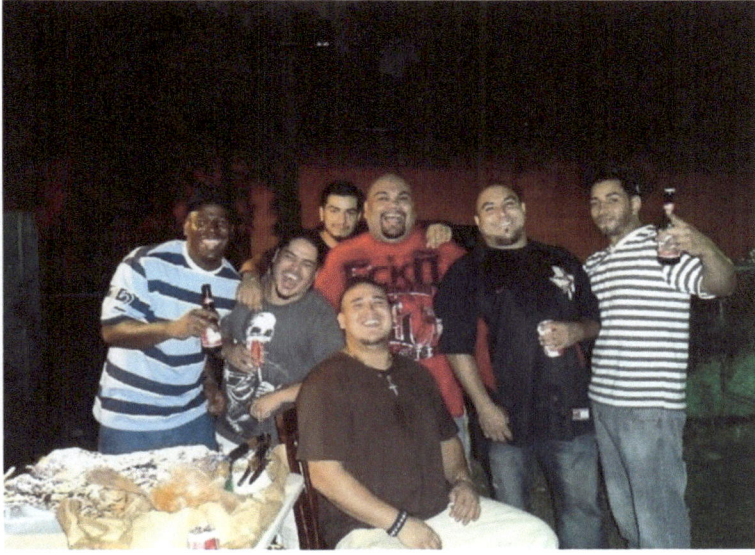

Me and My boys Chris, Greeneyes, Jay and Tocayo

Chris and I

Chuco and I

My Children Emry, Edward, Destiny and I

My Sisters Kimberly, Gayle, and I

Me with My Homies Tocayo and Boy

My Older Sisters, Gayle (R.I.P., I love you) and Cynthia aka DJ Eque and I

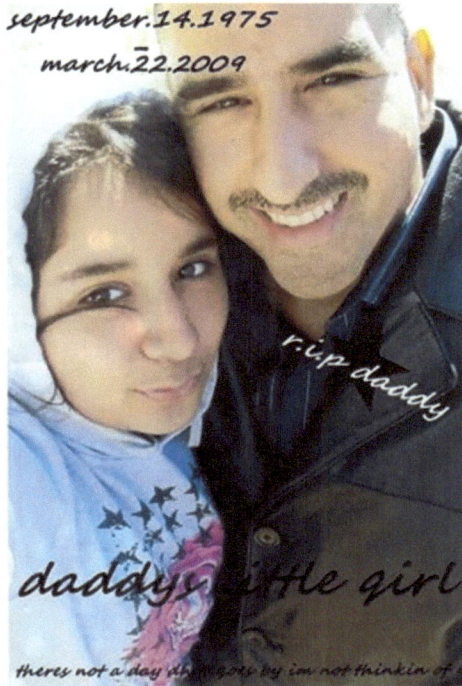

september.14.1975
march.22.2009

r.i.p daddy

daddys little girl

theres not a day that goes by im not thinkin of

My Friend From School, Rene T. R.I.P.

CHAPTER FIVE

People have a right to think for themselves and not everyone joins a gang for the reasons I've outlined. Everyone has choices, but I am trying to shed light on the conditions in the community that affect these choices. When asked why they joined a gang, most gang members will avoid going into their feelings. They will give you all these small reasons and avoid main reasons. Many times they don't even understand the main reasons, so it becomes harder for counselors and other professionals to communicate with them. I was a gang leader for a long time and I've heard all of the excuses.

The Environment: Many gang members will tell you that the environment around them made them join a gang. While it is true that your surroundings influence your decisions, we don't have to be products of our environment. This is why proper parenting is so important. Everything comes back to the parents, and as I stated earlier, the environment only influences you negatively if the parents fail to provide proper attention, direction and love.

The environment where you live at may be full of gangs. You may see them in the streets, the schools, the parks and even the libraries. If a child has no sense of direction and wanders around the streets looking for something to do, who do you think they are going to eventually run into? Not a role model, I can tell you that.

You do not have to join a gang because of where you live. Your environment doesn't have to make you who you are. There are many people who come from bad environments who have never considered joining a gang. Families live in the environments they can afford to live in, but whether rich or poor you still have a choice about how you will conduct yourself. Joining a gang is a choice not a requirement. If the kids in your environment were jumping off of tall buildings onto the concrete, breaking their bones, would you follow them just because you're from that environment? I don't believe you would, so why do you have to follow them into a gang? Joining a gang is like slow suicide. You never know when you're going to have to take a bullet, either from your enemy's gun or or from someone in your own gang. I've seen gang members tell each other they love each other one minute and then kill each other over a woman in the next. The choices you make determine your future. You have control over your destiny.

I'm not saying you can always avoid and ignore gangs; in some neighborhoods, that's impossible. What I'm saying is that you can choose to not affiliate yourself with them. You don't have to accept their invitations to go anywhere or do anything with them. You can find friends at school that don't live in your environment and do things with them. You can play sports or join after school programs. If they don't have any after school programs where you live, you can work on creating one. You can create your own alternatives to a gangster lifestyle. Why risk your life for a group of people that don't care if you live or die? Ask yourself that question over and over again before you decide to join a gang because of the environment you live in.

Making Money: Many people try to make money illegally not because they are bad people, but because they want to contribute to their household and jobs are scarce in poor neighborhoods. Still there are others who just want to have nice material items. They want big cars with nice paint, rims and a booming system. They want to wear the finest clothes and jewels. Money can buy all of these things but it can't buy happiness, or your life back after your dead. Gangsters have their hustles, and sometimes gangsters can make money on the street faster than people who make money legally. But that's just what that money is, fast. In the long run, is it worth your life? This all goes back to the lack of proper attention, direction and love from the parents. Sometimes kids join gangs to get material items that their parents can't afford to give to them. Other times kids join gangs believing that the more money they bring into the house and give to their parents the more love they'll receive from them.

One of the saddest occurrences in the hood is when parents accept money from their kids who are in gangs without ever questioning where the money is coming from. Too many parents are willing to look the other way as long as they are receiving money from their child.
If you think you're doing a good thing by giving your parents money that you got from illegal activities, you're wrong! Having a legal hustle is always smarter in the long run. Don't risk getting killed or going to jail by joining a gang for the money. If you get killed right now, who do you think is going to pay for your funeral? Your family, not those gang members. Sure, they'll bring flowers, but I've never heard of a gang covering the funeral costs for one of their members.
Parents should let children know that material items are not important and that they don't need expensive things to be accepted by their peers. All a child needs to do is to be responsible, honest and have a good heart and people will accept them the way they are. Parents should continue to plant positive messages into their children's heads.
Parents should also encourage their children to look for a job if they

want to make their own money. If the child gets a job, the parents should express how proud they are, and if the child doesn't the parents should still express how proud they are at the attempt. I made fast money on the streets while I was in a gang, but it wasn't worth getting locked up away from my family for so long. The trouble you go thru to get that buck is never worth it. You have to watch out for rival gangs. You won't be able to go to certain neighborhoods to do business. As a young person of color I had to be careful not to be harassed by the police, but when I joined a gang I increased my chance of getting harassed until it was damn near guaranteed. When I was released from prison, I did what I had to do to make legal money. I worked at Popeyes. I went to Alvin Community College to learn how to be a mechanic. I did not accept failure, and I was determined not to get back involved with gangs and to not go back to jail.

Sometimes gangs have rules that state that a portion of any money made by gang members must go back to the gang. Having too many hands in the pot when dealing with illegal money will not only decrease your profit, it will also increase your chance of getting caught. Being in a gang will just draw more attention to you by the police and society in general. It makes it harder and more dangerous for you to make money. That was your sole purpose right? If you get busted making money illegally and go to prison, who do you think is going to send you money? Your gang might send you a little money here and there for about a year or two, but after that it will be your family supporting you as you're in prison doing a bunch of time. Trust me, they give out a lot of time for financial fraud, they don't care if it's your first time or not.

So to recap, let's say you joined a gang, started making money illegally which you used to support your family and yourself. You got busted and they sent you to prison. Now your family is in an even worst position. You are no longer able to help with the bills. Your family members now have to send you some of the little money they are making. That fast money seemed like the answer at the time, but your chances of getting arrested are high and when that happens you hurt your family in the long run, financially and emotionally. Make the right choice if you want to help your family and yourself. Joining a gang doesn't bring money, it brings trouble.

Family: Family ties can be a determining factor in a child's decision to join a gang. Many children join gangs because their brothers, mothers, fathers, aunts, uncles and even grandparents were also gang members. Children look up to the older people in the home and often want to follow in their footsteps. They see their older family members in a gang and they believe it's a family tradition. I'm sure parents don't want their children joining gangs, even ones that are proud to be in a gang themselves. How do we go about stopping this cycle? First, if you are a parent that is affiliated with gangs, try to distance yourself from that. Don't associate with gang members or have them in your home. Don't dress like a gang member. Let's think about our children. Let's not give them the impression that this is the way life has to be. You really don't want your children joining a gang because you know the danger and outcomes of it. Let's be better role models and parents to our children. Let's stop this cycle. You don't want your children to end up dead or locked-up for a long time for something stupid.

Parents, if you really love your kids and care about them, you will do everything in your power to protect them from becoming a victim to gangs. Let's start by stopping the cycle in our own home.

Peer Pressure: This is a concern among many children. Peer pressure is one of the leading reasons why children do things they may not want to do, including joining gangs. What happens often is that your child has a friend that joins a gang, so this friend begins to try and influence your child to do the same. Your child really doesn't want to join the gang because he or she knows the trouble that comes with it, but your child may also value this friendship. This friend continues to pressure your friend into joining the gang regardless, and children can sometimes value the opinion of their peers over the common sense of their parents. This is why parents must know exactly who their children are friends with. Parents should pay attention to changes in their child's behavior. Pay attention to the clothes your children wear, they way they talk. Parents should also talk openly to their children about the perils of peer pressure. It is not easy to resist sometimes.

Protection: A desire for protection is one of the main tools gangs use to recruit new members. They scout for kids who are having problems with bullies at school. If they see a kid getting picked on they will say "if you join my gang, you will never have problems with these bullied or anyone else." This is a common and effective tactic. The truth is, gangs will only protect you to a point. If you are having a problem with a bully they will come to your rescue. However if it involves a drug dealer from the neighborhood or someone they like more than you, I guarantee that you will be on your own. Joining a gang for protection is stupid. They can't protect you from getting killed. They can't protect you from going to prison. They can't protect you from getting beat up by a different gang when you're at the mall shopping. They can't protect your house or car from getting shot-up. Joining a gang will bring you destruction, not protection. So think before you join a gang and ask yourself this question-

"Am I willing to sacrifice my life and the lives of my family members for a group of people that really don't care anything about me?" The only things gangs protect are their own investments.

Attention: Sometimes children join gangs for nothing more than attention. This goes back to the lack of attention, direction and love from parents. If children don't get it at home they will go and find it somewhere else. Gangs love attention. They love to be on the news, that's like advertisements to them. It's true that if it's attention you are looking for, you will certainly receive it by joining a gang. You will receive attention from the cops. You will receive attention from rival gangs. Nothing positive ever comes out of joining a gang. You will be trying to duck and dodge the bullets that are fired at you. You will be labeled a criminal by society. I'm sure this is not the type of attention you were looking for. You want some attention? Do some volunteer work at a hospital. Join a church in your neighborhood. There is a huge difference between positive and negative attention. Which one do you prefer?

Boredom: They say an idle mind is the devil's playground. Children's brains are busy, and if you don't keep them occupied they will get bored very easily. This is due to lack of love, direction and attention from their parents at an early age. Imagine your children are at home with nothing to do. You have your own set of stress to deal with so you tell your child to go outside and play. The child goes out into the streets looking for something to do and sees a group of people they recognize from school. Before you know it your child is being introduced to a gang. This introduction opens up a door that may eventually lead your child into joining that gang, but the problem started at home. If you give your child direction and attention they probably won't feel the need to join a gang. As parents we must give our children a sense of direction, attention, and love or they will look for it somewhere else. Try keeping your child busy with constant activity from an early age. Have your child play baseball or football. Introduce them to swimming or your favorite music. A child busy with positive activities will not have time to even think about joining a gang.

Once a child is involved in positive activities the parents must continue to stay involved. Go to games and even practices. Try to be there for as much as you can. Continue to be involved in your child's activities on a regular basis, throughout the school year. Many parents stop being involved in their children's activities when the child becomes a teenager. Most kids join gangs between the ages of 13 and 18 years old. The teenage years are when children are most influenced by their peers. So if you don't want your child to join a gang, put him or her in some kind of positive activity that will take up most of their free time, and continue to be involved.

CHAPTER SIX

When it comes to solving the problems that come with gangs I've heard many theories, and some of them are so off I just shake my head. Gangs are like the common cold. There is no cure for the common cold, you just have to wait it out. Sure, you can take medicine that treats the symptoms, but once you have a cold it is too late to go back and prevent the cause.

You can reduce the growth of gangs by stopping the cycle. We have to figure out how to stop the children from joining the gangs and eventually gangs will fade away. Parents must talk to their children about the dangers of gangs from an early age, especially if they are being raised in an environment prone to gang violence. . We have to reach the hearts and minds of our children before the gangs do. It is very hard to get out of a gang once you join one, so we must give our children the tools they need to resist a gangster lifestyle. Parents will save themselves a lot of worry and heartache by teaching their children the real about gangs.

One of the worst things a parent can say to a child is "do what I say, not what I do." There are parents that tell their children not to smoke, but smoke every day. They tell their children not to drink, but they drink every day. They tell them not to curse but they curse all the time. Why would children listen to you when you're doing the same things you're telling them not to do? Parents, let's start practicing what we preach. Children learn from observation.

I've written a lot about parental responsibility, but there is only so much parents can do. Taking personal responsibility is important. Even if your neighborhood is full of gangs, there are ways to avoid them. Gang members hang out in bunches. They like to be seen by numbers, so they are easily recognizable. If you see a friend of yours with a gang, don't go over to talk with him. Let him come to you if anything. That will show that you don't want to get to know the rest of their group.

"Where did I go wrong?" This is the question that parents ask themselves after they find out that their child is in a gang. It's easy to blame your parents for every negative thing that happens in your life. "My parents weren't there for me. My parents are gang members themselves. My parents this and my parents that." These are excuses. Yes, your parents have a responsibility but so do you. Look in the mirror; that is the only person responsible for your actions. You may not have "good" parents. Some parents just don't know how to be good parents because they were never taught how or because they had bad parents themselves. Does that mean you should join a gang because you have bad parents? No!! When you stop blaming your parents for your actions you can begin to grow. You have to learn from your parent's mistakes and push to do better, not worse than they did. Your life is far too valuable to waste it on a gang. You can turn a negative situation into a positive outcome if you just believe in yourself.

Children need to listen to their parents. If drug users tell you not to do drugs because they destroy you, they are telling you from experience. Parents also speak from this well of experience, so when they tell you not to join a gang, not to smoke, not to drink or do drugs it's because they already know the outcome of these things in the long run.

Another way to avoid gangs is to find a couple of friends that live outside of your neighborhood and go to their houses to hang out. Sign up to for sports, either at school or at the park. This will keep you occupied most of the time. Focus on family activities. You don't need to hang with a lot of people to have fun, so get yourself a few good friends that are on your level. Find a church you relate to and get involved in church activities. You will be amazed by how much fun you can have and how good it can feel to be involved with the church.

Being involved with gangs is like playing Russian roulette. You never know when you will be lying down in a casket or sent to prison for the rest of your life. I'm a living example of an ex-gang member sentenced to 20 years for killing a younger gang member. By the grace of God, I only received 20 years, but the other gang member wasn't so lucky; he's dead. I regret ever being in a gang and I deeply regret the pain I caused to that young man's family. These regrets made me decide to dedicate my life to not only trying to stop kids from joining gangs, but also to helping existing gang members to get out and do something more positive with their lives.

Many times you will hear gang members refer to their gang as their friends or family. I would say this is far from the truth. What is a friend, really? A friend is a person that will comfort you. A friend will not turn his back on you. A friend wouldn't want to see you get hurt or killed. A friend would do all he can to help you get out of trouble. These are just some of the qualities of a friend.

There isn't any true friendship between gang members. You may think these people are your friends, but upset the leader of the gang and your so called friends will be kicking your butt on command. You know this is the truth. There are gang members in the same gang that don't even like each other. Are you willing to die for someone that doesn't even like you? That's like selling your soul to the devil. The devil hates you but you are still willing to serve him. If you get caught doing illegal activities with your gang members and the D.A. threatens you all with a lot of time, chances are gang members will begin to blame each other to save their own skin. Believe me, I know from experience. It's part of the reason why so many young gang members are locked up now. They were trying to be loyal to their gang while someone from their gang was telling on them.

What kind of friend would put another friend in a life or death situation? Anytime you join a gang you are placing yourself in a life or death situation. With friends like these, who needs enemies?

Are gang members really your family? In my experience, many gang members don't even know each others first and last names, yet they call each other "family." Often, gang members don't even know where their fellow gang members live, because most gang members don't take you to their homes. When you get into trouble and locked up for a long period of time, will your fellow gang members write letters and send you money on a constant basis? Probably not! Once, I got arrested and needed two thousand dollars bail money so I could get out and fight my case. My sister Gayle asked many of my ex-gang "family" members to put up some of the money. There were over one hundred and fifty members in my ex-gang. One of them gave Gayle one hundred dollars. The rest of the money came from my real family and my real friends that weren't in gangs. One of the gang members asked Gayle why should he give me bail money when I was going to end up in prison in the long run anyway, and this was a guy I had risked my life for. That doesn't sound like family to me. I never talked to that guy again but it's my fault for trusting people that really didn't really care about me. Don't put yourself in the same situation. Gangs are not your family. Gangs do not love you, they use you.

I understand that when many children join gangs it's because they really don't know what's involved. But after being in the gang seeing your fellow members get killed or sent to prison, why do you these children remain? Nobody wants to die for something stupid. Nobody wants to be sent to prison for the rest of their life. Once you know the consequences of being a gang member, once you see the innocent people getting killed because of gang violence, you must be responsible for your actions. You must know that your actions may lead to your real family getting killed. Other gangs may do drive –by's on your home or shoot up your car just because you are in a different gang. Do you blame the other gangs for shooting up your house and car? Do you blame the other gangs for trying to kill you or your family? No!! You must blame yourself because you knew the consequences of being in a gang. That's what gangs do, attack their enemies with no regret.

CHAPTER SEVEN

There is an old West African fable about a frog and a scorpion. A scorpion wanted to cross over to the other side of a pond, but could not swim. So the scorpion decided to ask a frog to take him to the other side of the pond. The frog said to the scorpion "No, because you will sting me." The scorpion then asked the frog "why would I sting you in the middle of the pond causing us to both drown?" So the frog thought to himself and said that the scorpion had a point. The frog let the scorpion jump on his back and he began to swim across the pond. As they got to the middle of the pond, the scorpion stung the frog. The frog asked the scorpion, "why did you sting me?" The scorpion responded, "you knew I was a scorpion." The moral of the story is the scorpion did what he was supposed to do, sting and kill. That's his nature. The frog on the other hand had a choice not to take the scorpion on to the other side of the pond. The frog knew it was in the scorpion's nature to sting. He knew the consequences of his actions, yet still ignored them. What happened to the frog is not the scorpion's fault.

This story also applies to gangs. When you house or car gets shot up by a gang, that is the nature of the gang, it's what they do. If you are still in a gang and haven't been sent to jail, hurt, or been killed yet, you still have a choice. You can choose to not be in a gang. Remember, gangs attack other gangs most of the time. So ask yourself, "Why am I still in a gang?"

When kids join gangs they never think about the future. When you joined a gang what where you trying to accomplish? What was your future as a gang member? Let me be the one to tell you, there is no future in a gang, only consequences. The outcome is always negative. You cannot live a peaceful life as a gang member.

As I talk to older gang members in prison, none of them see a future in joining a gang. They say things like, "I'm an O.G., I've been in a gang a long time and don't have anything to show for it but imprisonment." You need to start using your brain and grow up. Do something that will help you in life, not destroy you. Give yourself a chance to have a future in life. Ask yourself "Why am I still in a gang?"

Many people say they choose to remain in gangs out of a sense of loyalty to an oath or commitment. I just laugh when they say that. How many oaths and commitments have you made in life that have been broken? I know you made plenty of promises to your parents that you broke as soon as they turned their backs. I know you've made commitments to your girlfriend, boyfriend, wife or husband that you did not keep. Some gangsters make oaths in court and lie to judges to keep themselves from going to jail. There's no future in gangs, grow up. When I say "grow up" I don't mean physically, I mean mentally. Remember, by you being in a gang you might stop your kids or family members from having a future. Their lives might be shortened by your gang affiliation.

I've experienced the prison life and realized that there is so much more to life than being in prison. I've come to understand that by being in a gang, I wasn't living at all. I was living bait, waiting for someone to take my life. Who wants to get killed or thrown in prison? These are the consequences of being in a gang. I've heard many gang members say, "If it's my time to die, then it's my time. I can't stop it." That's true, but you can greatly reduce the chances of an untimely death by keeping yourself away from dangerous situations. If you put yourself in a position to be killed, then you might get killed. But if you surround yourself with positivity you will see positive results.

Everybody has a destiny but you can change or run towards your destiny with your decision making. I've seen a lot of young people that will never be let out of prison because of poor decisions. Each one of them will tell you that if they had another chance they would have never joined a gang. Gang life is a sure fire road to death and imprisonment.

Is it too late to change your life? When I was in a gang, I used to always tell myself that a gang member is all I will ever be. I had no sense of direction. Living violently, ducking and dodging bullets and going to jail was all I did. I thought this violence was my way of life. I used to tell myself that it was too late for me to change, that I've lived this way for too long. What else do I know besides gang bangin?

It's never too late to make a change. There is a better life style than being in a gang. I know many ex-gang members who have became successful people once they made key changes to their life styles. All it took was a little push to get them on the right track. As I'm writing this book, I'm in college for four different trades. I've changed my life style so I know you can do the same. When a person is willing to change and do good, people are willing to help that person achieve that goal. There are support groups, youth advocates, and different types of people that are more than willing to help you change your life style and get you back on track. Do not ever believe it's too late to change. If you want to live in peace within yourself and avoid a lot of unnecessary trouble, change your life style. It feels great not to worry about drive-bys and shoot-outs. Ask yourself- do you want to live to die, or do you want to change your life style so that you can enjoy life?

www.ingramcontent.com/pod-product-compliance
Lightning Source LLC
Chambersburg PA
CBHW041227270326
41934CB00001B/26